YOU & YOUR CHILD
NUMERACY

Sarah Carvill

Consultant: Paul Broadbent

Letts

Contents

Words in **bold** are defined in the glossary at the back of this book.

"Do not confine your children to your own learning for they were born in different time."

HEBREW PROVERB

Dear Parent,

What happens at nursery and in primary school is vital to your child's education. What you do at home is just as important.

It's never too soon to start supporting your child's learning. The time that you spend with your child, reciting rhymes and playing with numbers, gives him or her a foundation that lasts a lifetime. Make the most of every opportunity for you and your child to enjoy learning together. You can give your child a real gift by teaching him or her to read numbers before the first year of school.

You don't need to be an expert. You do need to be enthusiastic. The time you invest at home – using maths skills in the kitchen, in the park, out shopping or in the car – will help your child achieve all through primary and secondary school.

This book is one in a major new series from Letts. It will help you support your child, with information about how children learn to use and understand number skills. It tells you how schools help children gain these basic skills, and advises on how you can help your child progress.

I hope you enjoy sharing the skills of numeracy with your child. The important thing is to make learning fun!

Roy Blatchford.

ROY BLATCHFORD
Series editor

What is numeracy?

What is mathematics?

Mathematics is the study of numbers, quantity and space. It is taught in school through daily lessons. An understanding of mathematics is needed in everyday life to help perform even the simplest tasks.

What is numeracy?

Numeracy is a key life skill. Being numerate means being able to solve number problems, including those to do with measuring, money and time. For example, being numerate means you can work out the score in a game of snooker or darts, handle the monthly household budget or measure up a room for wallpaper.

Parent tips and quotes

"I was always terrified of numbers and maths as a kid. When Ben started his maths classes we both got really involved in his workbooks and really enjoyed studying with him!"

"The times tables are so important to get right."

What is the National Numeracy Strategy?

The **National Numeracy Strategy** is a system of training and support for teaching mathematics in schools in order to raise the standards in mathematics. It will improve standards of numeracy through Daily Maths Lessons, including lots of mental and oral work, for all primary age children. The aim of the National Numeracy Strategy is that children should become numerate and confident enough to tackle mathematical problems independently.

Helping your child to become numerate requires a partnership between you and your child's school. This book will explain all about mathematics and numeracy skills and how you can help your child develop them.

Is my child numerate?

Although your child's age and experience determine his or her level of numeracy, it is possible to check if he or she is progressing well.

Ask yourself these questions:

- ✔ Is my child interested in numbers?

- ✔ Does my child think he or she is good at adding/counting etc.?

- ✔ Does my child enjoy puzzles and games that involve numbers?

- ✔ Can my child tackle a maths problem without immediately asking for help?

- ✔ Does my child notice patterns in numbers?

- ✔ Can my child see mathematical links in everyday activities?

If you answer 'Yes' to most of these questions, your child is already becoming numerate. If not, remember that all children develop at different rates.

Before your child starts school

You are your child's first teacher. He or she will be finding out things at home with you as you go about your daily routines. Your child's earliest ideas about maths will come through doing everyday activities with you and your family. Although children are not expected to do formal sums before they start school, maths learning can start very young!

Your child will see you counting out apples in the supermarket, measuring wallpaper, filling the car with petrol and using timetables when catching a train. As you do all these things you will be using mathematical skills that your child will pick up.

If your child becomes confident with maths at this stage, it will help him or her progress throughout school.

REMEMBER

- Maths can be fun and everyone can join in.
- Maths is around us all the time – everyday experiences can be learning opportunities.
- You do not have to be an expert – just enthusiastic.
- Helping your child need not be expensive – your time is more valuable.

A teacher's tips

✔ Listen to and watch your child. You will find out what he or she can already do.

✔ Build your child's confidence – praise and rewards are great boosters.

✔ Turn activities into games and make them fun.

✔ Let your child explore – there is often more than one way of doing something.

✔ Encourage your child to join in with you when shopping, cooking etc.

✔ Stop if your child gets bored.

Can I give my child a head start?

There are many informal ways to give your child his or her first experiences of mathematical ideas and concepts. If your child has encountered these before starting nursery, pre-school or primary school it will be easier for him or her to progress in formal learning later on.

These are the key areas to cover:

- ✔ counting

- ✔ recognising numbers

- ✔ writing numbers

- ✔ adding and subtracting

- ✔ measuring

- ✔ shape and space

Counting words

Your child's first experience of numbers will be saying the names of numbers when counting. He or she may become muddled after the first few numbers, but with time and experience your child will get it right.

You can encourage this by counting out building blocks when playing, counting ducks on a pond or candles on a birthday cake.

Helpful hints for counting

- ✔ Count with your child.
- ✔ Say the names of numbers clearly.
- ✔ Show numbers to your child.
- ✔ Sing songs or rhymes with numbers in them.
- ✔ Read stories with numbers in them.
- ✔ Count objects in pictures and stories.
- ✔ Talk about numbers as much as you can in everyday activities.

Writing numbers

Your child will learn how to write the numbers that he or she has seen and heard spoken. He or she will begin to associate these written numerals with real life situations. You can help:

1 Show your child how to write the numbers.

2 Show one number at a time until your child is more confident.

3 Give your child large crayons or paint and large sheets of paper to practise writing numbers.

4 Then give your child smaller pens and pencils so he or she can get used to them.

5 Make a collection of your child's efforts alongside numbers cut out from birthday cards and magazines.

6 Don't worry if your child gets numbers the wrong way round at first. This can happen until a child is six or seven.

7 Ask your child to write numbers when scoring a game or helping to write the shopping list.

Counting and recognising numbers

A pre-school child will begin to recognise that numbers have something to do with counting. He or she may spontaneously point numbers out to you. You can use these opportunities to talk about numbers further.

+ Your child will recognise numbers that are important – for example your door number or his or her age.

+ Your child will be able to recognise these numbers elsewhere – for example on a clock, a calendar or a car number plate.

+ Your child will start to see numbers in order – for example counting up to 9 on a telephone key pad.

+ You can also show your child large numbers that appear in telephone directories and TV commercials or on tape measures.

Adding and subtracting

Your child will begin to understand that adding or subtracting makes a quantity bigger or smaller. He or she will start to learn words that help with adding and subtracting.

Your child will add or subtract by adding one or taking away one. Ask him or her how many people there will be at the table when another person sits down, or when someone leaves the table. Your child will be able to do this by counting the number of people. He or she will then know that one more than three is four, without having to count up each time.

Encourage your child to use his or her fingers to show numbers that make ten. If your child holds up six fingers and then four more he or she will see it makes ten. Also by folding down fingers, when taking away from ten, your child can count how many are still up.

You can see if your child is learning to add and subtract if he or she is:

✔ using language such as 'more than', 'take away', 'the same as'

✔ counting shoes, socks or gloves in pairs

✔ counting the spots on dice in a game

✔ telling you how many there are when you add or take away objects

✔ saying how many more plates are needed on the table

✔ responding to questions when you ask for more or fewer objects

Measuring

When your child's vocabulary is developing, he or she will begin to learn words that relate to the size, weight or quantity of things.

Your child will begin to say words such as 'long', 'tall', 'wide' and 'short' and to associate them with objects. For example: 'This is the *short* carrot.'

Then your child will start to compare two things by using 'than'. For example: 'My hair is shorter *than* my gran's.'

When playing with toys or doing everyday activities your child will recognise that some objects which are the same can be different sizes. He or she will start to put these in order, for example: 'The biggest shoes are for dad, then the next ones are for my big brother and the smallest ones are for me.'

A the next stage of learning about measure your child will be able to match basic measuring words to situations, for example kilograms to weight.

Measuring time is an essential everyday skill. If your child has started to learn about time he or she will cope more easily with a routine on starting school, although telling the time is not something all children at **Key Stage One** can do.

Time

Your child will be able to have experience of time in a variety of ways.

✔ Remind your child of his or her age and show him or her the date and month on a calendar.

✔ Show your child the birthdays of family members on a calendar and tell their ages.

✔ Teach your child the days of the week and the months of the year. Cut up old calendars to use as cards for ordering and sorting.

✔ Match activities you do to the time on a clock. Use a clock face (analogue) and a digital clock.

✔ Use words like 'yesterday', 'next week', 'soon' etc. so that your child starts to understand when things happen and how time is ordered.

✔ Ask your child questions about when things are happening, for example: 'Will we have breakfast before we get dressed?' or 'Is lunchtime after bedtime?'

Shape and space

Young children are surrounded by images on pictures, in books and on television. They start to recognise that certain things have similar shapes. Your child will start to describe objects using mathematical words such as 'round', 'flat' and 'circle'. Useful activities that your child can do to help with understanding of shape include fitting shapes together, making patterns and looking at differences between shapes or objects.

The most important thing to remember when helping your child before he or she starts school is to make activities fun.

Handy shape and space resources

✔ jigsaws (bought or home-made by cutting up pictures)

✔ puzzles

✔ printing blocks (sponge shapes, cut potatoes, empty boxes) and paint

✔ collections of household objects which are the same shape

✔ shape stencils and templates for drawing round

✔ construction kits and building blocks

Activities should be games not chores!

Numeracy in the Early Years

What will my child do in pre-school or Reception?

Much of maths is to do with numbers, but it also involves measuring, shape and space and **data handling**. Your child will learn all about these and will be doing maths while playing and having fun.

YOUR CHILD WILL LEARN HOW TO:

- use graphs, charts and symbols to find out information

- use words associated with length, weight, time, money and **capacity**

- use construction kits and shapes

- measure and count with water, sand and in the home corner

Parent quote

"Before I chose my child's nursery I had a good look round. I especially looked for opportunities for my child to develop mathematical skills."

What should I look for in my child's Reception class or pre-school?

1 Are there areas for sand and water play?

2 Are there displays of numbers, charts and shapes on the walls?

3 Are there building blocks, construction kits and games?

4 Is there a home corner well equipped with a variety of food packaging, kitchen equipment and dolls?

Will my child have maths lessons?

When your child is at pre-school he or she will not have formal maths lessons that involve children sitting down 'doing maths'. Your child will learn maths through play, exploring, investigating and talking. The leader or teacher may set up particular activities with a maths focus, for example: 'Find out which cup holds the most water' or 'What is the tallest tower you can build?'

There will also be times when all of the children share maths together:

✔ listening to stories that involve numbers, counting or mathematical language

✔ singing number songs and rhymes

✔ talking about numbers, for example: 'Everyone show 4 fingers'

✔ showing work to the class and talking about it, for example a picture of printed shapes

✔ measuring the playground

✔ making models and cutting and sticking

✔ finding the right size clothes from the dressing-up box

Equipment for maths activities

✍ sand and water

✍ objects for counting

✍ different sized containers

✍ clocks and calendars

✍ number stencils, cards and charts

✍ flat and solid shapes

✍ building and construction kits

✍ money

✍ food packaging

✍ games

✍ modelling materials

✍ scales and tape measures

What will my child be learning?

LEARNING ABOUT NUMBERS

Your child will start to say the number words in order but may become muddled after the first few. He or she will learn to say them in the right order and will eventually count backwards as well as forwards.

ACTIVITIES IN THE EARLY YEARS

Teachers will plan how they teach about numbers. They will use mathematical language and encourage your child to do the same. Your child will learn about numbers mostly in games, rhymes and stories. He or she will then count out objects and match them to numbers.

Your child will have the chance to solve number problems in his or her head. He or she will start to draw pictures to show numbers and will then use many types of pencils and crayons on different surfaces to practise writing numbers and to learn to recognise their shapes.

Number practice

✔ count in 10s

✔ count on in 1s from 20

✔ count backwards

✔ point to numbers as you are counting

✔ show fingers to match a number

✔ point to and say numbers around the house

Parent quote

"We always translate the maths into something he can relate to. We give it meaning, not something he has no experience of."

Using numbers

As children become more confident with numbers, they can begin to use them. Beware – doing written sums too soon can confuse them and put them off learning more about numbers! To begin with, sums need to be in real situations and talked about rather than written.

ADDING AND SUBTRACTING

At first children may not understand a question such as: 'What is four add one?' At this stage in the early years of their education they link numbers with objects. So they will understand: 'There are four oranges on the plate. I put one more orange on the plate. How many oranges are there now?'

The next stage children reach is solving problems like this in their heads without needing to count objects.

Number language

As children become more numerate they begin to develop the language necessary to tackle mathematics:

- ✍ one, two, three . . .

- ✍ first, second, third . . .

- ✍ a hundred, a thousand . . .

- ✍ how many altogether, more than, add, count

- ✍ less than, take away, fewer

Adding and subtracting tips

- ✔ Add and subtract in real-life situations.

- ✔ Encourage learning patterns with numbers, for example 'one and one is two, two and two is four'.

- ✔ Use a variety of language, such as 'altogether', 'how many left' and 'one more'.

- ✔ Encourage your child to work out problems in his or her head, firstly using 'one more' or 'one less than'.

- ✔ Let your child draw pictures to show 'how many'.

- ✔ Don't write sums until your child is very confident talking about and explaining what he or she is doing.

- ✔ Don't worry about writing =, - and +. Talking is much more useful.

Measuring

Your child will begin by using very simple language such as 'big' and 'little' when talking about size or weight. In the Early Years your child will learn more words to do with measuring. At pre-school he or she will have the chance to use the new words when measuring objects and talking about them to other children or adults.

Your child will learn to compare.
- My cat *is smaller than* your dog.
- This block *is heavier than* that one.
- This bottle *holds more water than* your cup.

Your child will learn to put things in order.
- This doll is the *smallest*.
- My dad is the *tallest* person in the family.
- We are in the home corner *after* painting.

Your child will learn words for measuring things.
- My shoe is *size 8*.
- We bought *a pint* of milk.
- I am *80 centimetres* tall.

Your child will learn about measuring equipment.
- The *clock* shows when it is lunchtime.
- The flour is weighed on the *scales* when we make chapatis.
- We measured our sunflowers using a *tape measure*.

Parent quote

"We used to play 'sort out the shopping' with Jenny. She'd put the cans, the packets, the bottles and the jars in separate piles."

Measuring language

✎ big, greater, taller, larger

✎ small, lower, thinner, shorter

✎ first, next, last

✎ weight, length, time, capacity

✎ kilograms, grams, pounds

✎ metres, centimetres, miles

✎ litres, millilitres, pints

✎ day, week, month, year, age

✎ minutes, seconds, hours

Shapes and where things are

In your child's pre-school there will be lots of opportunities for gaining a sense of shape or space.

Your child will:

✔ fit shapes together when doing jigsaws, making patterns or using building blocks

✔ fit shapes in spaces when packing, tidying up or putting on shoes

✔ sort shapes when printing with circle shapes only, looking for triangles around the classroom or making models out of boxes

✔ describe where things are when finding two different ways to the book corner, showing that the slide is beside the climbing frame or describing the journey to school

Remember

✔ Be aware of the activities that take place in your child's nursery or playgroup.

✔ Sing songs and say number rhymes.

✔ Practise writing numbers.

✔ Use mathematical words so your child can copy you.

✔ Involve your child in activities around the home which involve maths.

✔ Do an activity at home that your child enjoys at pre-school.

Shape and space language

✐ square, triangle, circle

✐ corner, edge, side

✐ flat, round, curved, straight

✐ cube, box, ball, cone

✐ next to, between, underneath

Show an interest in any work your child brings home and find out what he or she did at school.

The National Numeracy Strategy

The National Numeracy Strategy (NNS) was launched in primary schools in September 1999. It gives primary school teachers guidelines for the teaching of mathematics to children from Reception to Year 6.

Schools are being provided with training and support, through the National Numeracy Strategy, in order to reach targets set by the government. The target for 2002 is for 75% of 11-year-olds to reach the expected standard for their age by the end of their primary education.

The aim of the NNS is to provide children with the key life skill of numeracy.

How can I become involved in the National Numeracy Strategy?

As part of the National Numeracy Strategy your child's school will be promoting higher standards of numeracy. This will involve all adults in school including the headteacher, teachers, classroom assistants, parents and governors. You will be kept well informed and encouraged to be involved through discussions at school and by working with your child at home.

Examples of out of class activities or homework for the NNS are:

- counting out the money in a purse or piggy-bank, or weighing different objects on a kitchen or bathroom scales
- playing a number game or puzzle
- learning number facts or multiplication tables by heart
- gathering information for use in the next lesson
- thinking about how to solve a problem
- preparing a contribution for a group presentation to the whole class

How will the National Numeracy Strategy affect my child's learning?

Since September 1999 schools have been providing a structured Daily Maths Lesson of approximately 45 minutes to 1 hour for all children of primary age. Your child's teacher will work with the whole class together for much of the time, and oral and mental work will feature strongly in each lesson.

The purpose of the NNS is for teachers to set high expectations for the children in your child's class and to help them understand how children should progress through the primary years.

The NNS guides teachers on how to plan and teach mathematics lessons and how to assess your child's progress. It also encourages the use of mathematics in other school subjects.

The NNS should help children to gain the confidence to tackle mathematics problems without needing help from a teacher.

The Daily Maths Lesson

How can I help my child get the most out of the Daily Maths Lesson?

1 Find out what your child's teacher is doing in class each week.

2 Go to any meetings the school holds to explain how the Numeracy Strategy is being taught in your child's class.

3 Buy or borrow books on mathematical topics or that contain numeracy activities for children.

4 Make a number line or 100 square to use at home. Ask the school what equipment you should buy, if any, for your child.

5 Try to spend some time on a regular basis working with your child on learning number facts.

6 Support your child with his or her homework.

7 Encourage your child to be a good listener and confident speaker about mathematics by working together at home.

What will my child be learning?

NUMBERS AND THE NUMBER SYSTEM

The Daily Maths Lesson will help children to:

✔ have a sense of the size of a number and where it fits into the number system

✔ know by heart number facts, such as number bonds, multiplication tables, doubles and halves

✔ use what they know by heart to work out answers in their heads

CALCULATIONS

The Daily Maths Lesson will help children to:

✔ work out answers accurately and efficiently, both mentally and with pencil and paper, using a range of methods

✔ recognise when it is appropriate to use a calculator, and be able to do so effectively

> ### Parent quote
>
> "When we heard about the Daily Maths Lessons we were really pleased that our children would be getting that special time to focus on maths skills. We've really noticed the improvement in both our children."

SOLVING PROBLEMS

The Daily Maths Lesson will help children to:

✔ make sense of number problems and know which methods are needed to solve them

✔ explain their methods and reasoning using correct mathematical language

✔ judge whether their answers are sensible and be able to check them where necessary

MEASURE, SHAPE AND SPACE

The Daily Maths Lesson will help children to:

✔ suggest suitable units for measuring and make sensible estimates of measurements

✔ explain and make predictions from the numbers in graphs, diagrams, charts and tables

Numeracy at Key Stage One

How much time will my child spend on mathematics each week?

Your child will have a Daily Maths Lesson lasting about 45 minutes every day. Your child's teacher will also plan numeracy related work in other subjects, for example collecting information in geography, measuring in science or looking at patterns in art.

WHAT FORMAT DO THE LESSONS TAKE?

Each lesson is divided into three parts:

Parent quote

"An ability in mental maths makes a big difference. I think all the work we put in with Tony really paid off."

1   Mental and oral (about 10 minutes). There is an emphasis on mental calculation and talking about numbers. This part of the lesson will allow your child to extend and practise his or her mental skills in maths.

2   Main activity (about 25 minutes). The teacher will work with the whole class, or with smaller groups of children, teaching something new. Your child will practise his or her skills and investigate ways of solving problems.

3   **Plenary** (5–10 minutes). During this session the teacher may revise something from the lesson, allow sharing of work or sort out problems from the lesson.

What will my child learn to do in Key Stage One?

There are four main areas your child will cover in the National Numeracy Strategy:

1 Numbers and the number system

2 Calculations

3 Solving problems

4 Measure, shape and space

Your child will also find out how these four areas are linked. A summary of each area is given on page 16.

A summary of each area is given on page 16.

How can I help my child in Key Stage One?

Your child will follow a structured curriculum in Key Stage One. In order to help him or her cope with the change from the Early Years there are ways you can help:

+ Find out what your child is doing in maths lessons.

+ Show an interest when your child is talking about his or her numeracy work and ask questions about it.

+ Help your child with any task he or she has been given to do at home.

+ Do activities at home similar to those your child is doing at school.

+ Play games that involve counting spaces on a board or using dice.

+ Use the opportunities provided by shopping trips, days out or cooking to talk about maths and solve problems.

Your child needs to learn addition and subtraction facts by heart, for example 14 + 6 = 20, 13 – 5 = 8. Knowing these without having to count out objects will help your child solve problems more quickly. It will also make numeracy more fun as your child will not have to spend time counting in order to solve every problem. Your child will also begin to learn multiplication facts (times tables) and division facts, for example 3 x 2 = 6, double 7 is 14, 8 ÷ 4 = 2.

Parent tips and quotes

"Children will continue to find some of the activities they did earlier in their education a lot of fun. Many activities can be extended to make them more of a challenge. They will still enjoy stories, songs and rhymes with numbers in them."

"We were really surprised by how interesting Kevin's numeracy work was. It even inspired my husband to take up evening classes!"

Games to help your child learn number facts

Write out a pair of cards with the sum on one card and the matching answer on the other.

e.g.

Make about ten pairs like this with different sums on. You could make different sets for addition, subtraction, multiplication and division.

Snap

Shuffle the cards and share them out among the players. Take turns to put a card down. When a sum matches an answer shout 'Snap!'. The player with most cards wins.

Pelmanism

Lay all the cards face down and spread them out on the table. Take turns to turn two cards face up. If the cards have a matching answer and sum the player keeps the pair. The winner is the player with most pairs.

How many sums?

Give your child a challenge to find as many sums as possible with the same answer.

You could give more points if your child gives a multiplication or division fact, or adds or subtracts three numbers.

Number hunt

Ask your child to find as many numbers as possible around the home, for example on the oven (not a hot one!), washing machine, car number plates etc.

Can your child see which is the greatest number?

Can your child put the numbers in order?

Can your child read each number in words? (For example: '428 is four hundred and twenty-eight.')

Towards the end of Key Stage One

As your child comes to the end of Year 2 (at or coming up to age 7) he or she will do the Key Stage One National Test in maths. Any time between January and May your child's teacher will check what he or she can do by assessment. This is covered more fully in Chapter Eight.

It is important that your child learns number facts in Key Stage One .

Numeracy at Key Stage Two

How much time will my child spend on mathematics each week?

Your child will have a Daily Maths Lesson of about 50 minutes to 1 hour every day. Your child's teacher will also plan opportunities for maths-related work in other subjects, for example drawing line graphs in science, finding average rainfall in geography, working out dates in history from a time line.

WHAT FORMAT DO THE LESSONS TAKE?

The lesson is divided into three parts:

1 Mental and oral (5–10 minutes). During this part of the lesson your child's teacher may get the class to practise skills, which may be needed later in the lesson. This might include:
   - counting in steps of different sizes, for example in 20s starting from 347
   - practising mental calculations, for example giving a number which is 3 more than a multiple of 6
   - working out new facts from facts already known, for example 7 x 2 = 14 so 70 x 2 = 140
   - reviewing a home activity
   - building on strategies
   - discovering ways of learning facts by heart

2 Main activity (30–40 minutes). During the main part of the lesson your child's teacher may work with the whole class, small groups, pairs or individuals. The activities in this part of the lesson will include:

- introduction of a new topic or going over or extending previous work
- developing vocabulary, using correct symbols and learning new terms
- using and applying concepts and skills learnt

3 Plenary (5–10 minutes). This is an important part of the lesson, as the teacher will take this chance to help children understand their achievements and work out where they have to go next. The plenary may also include:
- discussing and solving problems
- making links with previous work
- reminding children of their personal targets
- drawing together what has been learned
- groups or individuals presenting their work to the class

What will my child learn to do at Key Stage Two?

The National Numeracy Strategy is a structured way of teaching the National Curriculum for mathematics. There are three main areas your child will cover through the National Numeracy Strategy.

✔ Numbers and the number system

✔ Calculations

✔ Making sense of number problems

How can I help my child in Key Stage Two?

Your child will spend at least an hour of the school day doing mathematics. It is essential that any work done at home is mainly fun. There will be times, however, when your child has a formal homework activity, such as practising a written calculation or revising for a test.

Helping your child

✔ Find out what your child is doing at school and whether he or she has any concerns about the work.

✔ Show an interest by asking to see some of your child's work

✔ Check your child's homework and give advice where necessary.

✔ Test your child on tables and other number facts.

✔ Play games, such as Monopoly, chess or draughts, that require an understanding of mathematics.

✔ Be positive and encourage your child to discuss his or her work in a mature way.

It is still very important in Key Stage Two for your child to learn tables and other associated number facts to improve numeracy skills. The longer it is left, the more difficult it will be. Always try to make learning times tables fun!

How can I help my child learn the multiplication tables?

FLASH CARDS

Make sets of flash cards with a number fact and the answer on each one, for example 7 x 9 = 63. If your child has a good visual memory he or she may see the whole fact and remember it. Next make cards with just the facts on them, for example 7 x 9. Show your child a card and challenge him or her to say the answer as quickly as possible. Concentrate on one table at a time, then gradually mix up cards from different tables until your child knows all the facts.

PELMANISM

Make pairs of cards with a multiplication fact on one card and the answer on the other. Turn all the pairs of cards face down and muddle them up. Ask your child to turn over two cards. If the fact and the answer match your child wins the pair. Continue until all pairs are matched.

This game could be varied by introducing division facts, for example 27 ÷ 9 = 3. This card can then be matched with the cards 3 x 9 and 27 to make a trio.

Getting to grips with the multiplication tables

★ Show your child that once he or she knows one table, for example x5 then he or she will know at least one fact from all the other tables, for example 8 x 5 = 40 from the x8 table.

★ If your child knows the x2 table then the answers can be doubled for the x4 table, for example 3 x 2 = 6, so 3 x 4 = double 6 = 12. And once the x4 table is known the answers can be doubled for the x8 table.

This method can also be used from the x3 table to the x6 table and the x12 table.

These tricks will help your child learn some of the tables:

✔ The answers to the x5 and x10 tables have patterns of last digits.

✔ The x11 table follows a pattern of double digits up to 10 x 11, for example 2 x 11 = 22, 3 x 11 = 33, 4 x 11 = 44 and so on.

✔ The x9 table can be learnt in two ways:

1. Use the hands to show the digits of the answers.
To find out 3 x 9 your child should:
Hold hands out, palms facing inwards.
Work from the left and count from left to right.
Count the third finger along and fold it down.
The number of fingers to the left of the folded-down finger is the 10s digit i.e. 2.

The number of fingers to the right of the folded-down finger is the units digit i.e. 7. So 3 x 9 = 2 tens and 7 units = 27.

This method helps learn the facts. The more your child practises doing this, the quicker he or she will know the answers.

2. Ask your child to write out the x9 table. Can he or she see the patterns of numbers in the tens and units digits? What do the digits add up to each time?

That only leaves the x7 table. Knowledge of all the other facts will help your child have an idea of the size of the answers. He or she will also know all the x7 facts from the other tables which will make learning it much easier.

Different ways to learn

Multiplication tables can be written in two ways:

1 x 8 = 8	8 x 1 = 8
2 x 8 = 16	8 x 2 = 16
3 x 8 = 24	8 x 3 = 24 etc.

It will help if your child is familiar with both ways and understands how the facts could be shown in context – for example 2 x 8 could be 2 boxes of 8 pencils or 8 x 2 could be 8 pairs of shoes.

How do I know which written methods my child is being taught?

Your child will be introduced to a variety of written methods for doing calculations involving the four operations of addition, subtraction, multiplication and division. Some of these are shown on the following pages. The mental strategies your child has learnt will help him or her to understand the written methods and increase his or her speed and accuracy.

These are some of the standard methods for written and part mental/part written calculations:

ADDITION

★ Adding the most significant (greatest value) digits first.

$$
\begin{array}{r}
7587 \\
+ \quad 675 \\
\hline
7000 \\
1100 \\
150 \\
12 \\
\hline
8262
\end{array}
$$

1100 add mentally from
150 the top

★ Using 'carrying'.

$$
\begin{array}{r}
7587 \\
+ \quad 675 \\
\hline
8262
\end{array}
$$

1 1 1 1

SUBTRACTION

★ Counting back.

$$
\begin{array}{r}
754 \\
- \quad 286 \\
\hline
500 \\
- \quad 32 \\
\hline
468
\end{array}
$$

(754–254)
(286–254)

★ Decomposition.

$$
\begin{array}{rl}
754 & = \quad 700 + 50 + 4 \\
- \ 286 & \quad\ \ \underline{200 + 80 + 6}
\end{array}
$$

$$
= \quad 700 + 40 + 14 \qquad 754
$$
$$
\quad\ \ \underline{200 + 80 + \ 6} \qquad - \ 286
$$

leading to

$$
= \quad 600 + 140 + 14
$$

$$
- \quad \underline{200 + 80 + \ 6}
$$
$$
\quad\ \ 400 + 60 + 8 = 468
$$

MULTIPLICATION

★ Area method.

72 x 6

x	70	2		
6	420	12	=	432

★ Partitioning (long multiplication).

372 x 24

$$
\begin{array}{r}
372 \\
\times \quad 24 \\
\hline
1488 \\
7440 \\
\hline
8928
\end{array}
$$

(4 x 372)
(20 x 372)

DIVISION

★ Using multiples of the number being divided by.

$$256 \div 7 = (210 + 46) \div 7$$
$$= 30 + 6 \text{ remainder } 4$$
$$= 36 \text{ remainder } 4$$

★ Repeated subtraction.

$977 \div 36$

```
              27
         36) 977
            - 720  (36 x 20)
              257
            - 252  (36 x 7)
                5
```

Answer is 27 remainder 5 or 27 ⁵⁄₃₆

There are other methods taught by teachers for each of the four operations. If you have any doubts about the methods your child is being taught for written calculations check with his or her teacher.

Towards the end of Key Stage Two

As your child reaches the end of Year 6 (age 11) he or she will do Key Stage Two National Tests in maths. During May your child will take two papers, one with the use of a calculator and one without. There is more information about the National Tests in Chapter Eight.

Special needs and abilities

What are special educational needs?

A child is defined as having special educational needs (SEN) if he or she has a learning difficulty which needs special teaching. A learning difficulty means either that the child finds something much more difficult than most children of the same age, or that the child has a disability which needs different educational facilities from those that schools generally provide.

Children who need special teaching are not only those with obvious learning difficulties, such as those who are physically disabled, deaf or blind. They also include those whose learning difficulties are less apparent, such as slow learners and emotionally vulnerable children.

How do mainstream schools adapt to children with physical disabilities?

✔ The oral part of a lesson can be slowed down to accommodate children who are deaf or have a hearing impairment.

✔ Signing, symbols or special aids can be used to make communication easier.

✔ The length of tasks can be shortened for children who have a short concentration span or emotional or behavioural problems.

Will the National Numeracy Strategy help children with specific needs?

The Daily Maths Lesson is appropriate for almost all children. It focuses on the needs of all children and on what can be provided to improve their learning opportunities. The key aspects of the NNS are:

✔ giving greater emphasis to children's language during mathematics lessons

✔ encouraging children to learn by working together

The Daily Maths Lesson

✔ Children with special educational needs can benefit from working with and learning from more able children.

✔ Children with special educational needs can see and hear instant success in mental and oral work.

✔ The quick pace of lessons heightens the interest and increases the concentration span of children with special educational needs.

✔ There are many opportunities in the Daily Maths Lesson for children of different abilities to work in pairs or groups, sharing ideas.

✔ Although there is a need for written recording in numeracy, the emphasis is placed on mental and oral work which will benefit children who have difficulty writing.

✔ Children have the opportunity to do practical work which can also assist in other areas of their individual needs.

✔ The Daily Maths Lessons include mathematical games and puzzles which make learning fun!

Special needs children and numeracy

Children with special educational needs are encouraged to take part in the Daily Maths Lessons. They are encouraged to work with the rest of the class during the mental and oral session. The next activity may be adjusted to suit their particular needs. The final plenary session will greatly benefit SEN children as it can be a time for 'ironing out' problems, reviewing work done or resolving misunderstandings.

How will a child with SEN benefit in numeracy lessons?

The National Numeracy Strategy (NNS) much emphasises mental and oral work in the Daily Maths Lesson. Children are encouraged to talk and think about maths much more now than they used to be. This is the best way of ensuring that children gain a good grounding in numeracy.

Some schools teach mixed ability classes for maths, while others teach children in ability groups or sets. Check with your child's school how they organise maths teaching.

Questions to ask your child's teacher

✔ Are children taught maths in mixed ability classes or sets/groups?

✔ If my child is in a set, can he or she be moved depending on progress?

✔ Will the work in a mixed ability class be too difficult for my child?

✔ How is success monitored?

✔ How will my child's particular need be addressed in numeracy lessons?

What if my child has English as an additional language?

There are a number of different methods your child's teacher can use if your child has English as an additional language.

- The teacher will plan questions specifically for children at the earlier stages of learning English as an additional language.
- Your child's teacher will use flash cards or wall displays showing mathematical vocabulary if your child is not familiar with English.
- Your child will be given basic written instructions and explanations.
- Your child will have access to strong visual images such as number lines, 100 squares, drawings and charts.
- In whole class sessions your child will benefit from working with other children and adults and hearing them speak English.
- Your child will learn facts through repetition of numbers and counting in the oral part of the lesson.

Parent quote

"I have two children, one of whom has learning difficulties. I learnt early on not to compare them. They both achieve in different ways."

How do I know if my child is very able in mathematics?

Look out for these signs:

✔ Does your child deal with abstract maths easily and more quickly than other children of the same age?

✔ Does your child become bored quickly because work is too easy?

✔ Does your child solve mental maths problems quickly and accurately?

✔ Does your child recognise mathematics in everyday situations?

✔ Does your child prefer exploring numbers to other activities?

Gifted children

If your child is exceptionally gifted in mathematics the school may promote him or her to an older age group just for maths. This will allow your child the opportunity to discuss maths with children working at a similar level and may make it easier for your child to fit in with his or her peers.

How will my able child be taught numeracy?

Most children in your child's school will be taught with their own class, whether mixed ability or in sets. A more able child can be stretched through group work, harder problems for homework and extra challenges. These might include using **Information and Communications Technology**, for example using a **turtle**, or solving problems downloaded from the Internet.

Your child's teacher will direct more challenging questions to able children. Time is set aside each term for children to go over work, so if your child is very able he or she will spend the time carrying out an investigation which could be continued at home.

During normal daily lessons time is given over to children to practise and go over (consolidate) methods. An able child will need less time for this, and the teacher will provide interesting extra (extension) work for him or her.

Getting children to talk and think about maths ensures they gain a good grounding in numeracy.

> **Parent quote**
>
> "Our daughter is very able in maths. All she ever wanted to do was lots of complicated calculations. We encouraged her to have other interests as well so she had experiences to relate the maths to."

Formal testing

All children entering primary school in England and Wales undergo formal testing. This testing, known as **Baseline Assessment**, is carried out soon after your child starts school at five years old. You then have the opportunity to discuss your child's development with teachers at a parents' evening.

Many parents worry about the idea of testing five-year-olds and the effect it has on them. In fact, assessing children who are entering primary school is nothing new. Teachers have always looked at the skills and experience of each new child in order to understand his or her needs.

There are goals set for children's learning by the time they start compulsory education at the age of five. These goals have been agreed nationally to help parents and teachers have common expectations.

What does Baseline Assessment involve?

There are a number of assessment schemes for schools to choose from but all Baseline Assessment schemes cover:

✔ language and literacy

✔ mathematics

✔ personal and social development

Some schemes also cover physical development, knowledge and understanding of the world and creative development.

EARLY GOALS IN MATHEMATICS

Your child's teacher will assess him or her within seven weeks of starting school to see if he or she is able to:

✔ use mathematical language, such as 'circle', 'bigger' and 'in front of'

✔ describe shape, position, size and quantity

✔ recognise and recreate patterns. For example: circle, triangle, circle – what comes next?

✔ compare, sort and match everyday objects

✔ recognise and use numbers up to 10, for example counting or saying number rhymes

✔ recognise larger numbers from everyday situations

✔ use mathematical understanding to solve problems. For example: there are 4 saucers and 2 cups, so 2 more cups are needed

✔ understand and record numbers, for example writing the number symbol for a set of objects

✔ show early understanding of addition and subtraction and use appropriate language

✔ start to understand time and measure, for example knowing that home time is before tea, putting different shoes in order of size

---

Why have Baseline Assessment?

It is not the aim of Baseline Assessment to make judgements on ability, but to assess realistically what each child can and can't do. In this way teachers can plan for individual needs.

What are the National Tests?

Your child's school life is divided into Key Stages:
- Key Stage One starts in Year 1 (age 5-6) and finishes at the end of Year 2 (age 6-7).
- Key Stage Two starts when children enter Year 3 (age 7-8) and finishes at the end of Year 6 (age 10-11).

At the end of Year 2 and then again at the end of Year 6 your child will take the end of Key Stage assessment. It is made up of three elements:

- Tests
- Tasks
- **Teacher Assessment**

Why are the Key Stage One tests and tasks important?

Naturally, it is important that your child does as well as possible in the tests and tasks. Although the results do not determine what class your child will move up to in Key Stage Two, they do provide your child's next teacher with a picture of his or her overall attainment.

Key Stages

The National Curriculum is divided up into stages, each with work suited to the needs of your growing child.

Key Stage One	5-7 years old
Key Stage Two	7-11 years old
Key Stage Three	11-14 years old
Key Stage Four	14-16 years old

At the end of Key Stages One, Two and Three there are end of Key Stage assessments to find out about your child's progress up to this point.

The end of Key Stage One assessment

Between January and June of Year 2 all children will take tests and tasks in English and mathematics. These important tests assess the work your child has done during Key Stage One of the **National Curriculum**.

Your child will also have his or her work assessed by the teacher. The assessments will be set alongside your child's results in the tests and tasks to give a clear picture of his or her overall achievement.

The tasks and tests are carried out under the supervision of teachers in your child's school. They are also marked by the teachers. The results are then brought together for comparison by specialist teachers outside the school.

The tasks and tests help to find out what your child has learned. They also help you and your child's teacher to know whether your child has reached the national standards.

The tasks and tests will provide a brief summary in Year 2 of your child's attainment in specific aspects of mathematics, while teacher assessment is based on the full range of the work that your child has done during Key Stage One.

The school's report will explain to you what the results show about your child's progress, strengths and particular achievements, and will suggest targets for development. It will also explain why the task and test results may be different from the teacher's assessment.

Parent quote

"We found the teacher assessment much more helpful and encouraging than the rest of Preston's report."

What will my child do in a maths task?

Tasks are practical activities that your child may do in a small group or on his or her own while being observed by the teacher. The activities involve little or no recording but may involve your child talking with the teacher about the maths he or she is doing.

SAMPLE TASKS:

✔ place number cards in order of size

✔ discuss ways of sorting shapes

✔ continue a pattern of shapes and colours

✔ count two sets of cubes and give the total

If teachers think a child may have difficulties in the written test they will arrange for him or her to do tasks instead, in order to achieve the appropriate level.

What will my child do in the maths test?

Your child will do a test that will last about 45 minutes, although there is not an official time limit set for completion of the test. The test has questions about numbers, shape and space, measure and data handling.

The test questions vary in difficulty and topic throughout, and your child will be required to fill in answers in boxes, perform calculations and read information from charts.

WHAT KIND OF QUESTIONS ARE ASKED IN THE KEY STAGE ONE MATHS TEST?

1 Write these numbers in order, starting with the smallest.

35   2   97   152   14   79

2 Colour ¼ of this circle.

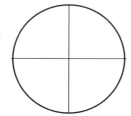

3 5 ice creams cost £1.00 altogether. How much does one ice cream cost?

Your child will complete as much of the paper as he or she can. There is no set time limit and your child will not be helped with the questions. The teacher can read words aloud that your child may find difficult but cannot read numbers or explain what words mean. Most children will take one paper covering Levels 2 to 3 of the National Curriculum. There are some different tasks and tests for different attainment levels. This is to ensure that children can be set a test or task in which they can show positive achievement.

Extension papers, with higher level questions taken from the end of Key Stage Two assessment, are also available for exceptionally able pupils.

How do I know how well my child has done?

The National Curriculum divides each subject into Levels 1 to 8. By the end of Key Stage One it is reasonable to expect that most children will be working between Levels 1 and 3. Level 2 is the level the majority of children are expected to reach. On very rare occasions a child may achieve Level 4 at the end of Key Stage One.

When your child's school has collected the results of their tasks and tests they will be reported to you at the end of July of the same year. Together with those results, you will receive the results of classroom assessments made by your child's teacher, based on the work your child has done during the school year. In addition you will be given a summary of the results for the other children in your child's school, and possibly for children nationally. This will help you know how your child is doing compared to other children of the same age.

Parent quote

"We were surprised by Emily's results. We thought she might have been put off by the formality of the testing, but she actually did very well."

How can I help my child prepare for the end of Key Stage One assessment?

There are several important ways in which you can help your child:

✔ Encourage your child to practise mathematics skills by asking questions in everyday situations.

✔ Work in a relaxed atmosphere – when you are *both* willing!

✔ Practise answering written questions – reading questions carefully and moving on to the next question if your child is stuck.

✔ Encourage your child to check his or her work.

✔ Don't say anything that may make your child anxious about the test.

✔ Don't criticise your child's efforts.

The end of Key Stage Two assessment

When your child is in the final year of Key Stage Two (Year 6, age 10–11), he or she will take written National Tests in English, mathematics and science. The tests are carried out in school, under the supervision of teachers, but are marked by examiners outside the school.

The tests will show what your child has learned in these key subjects. They also help parents and teachers to know whether children are reaching the standards set out in the National Curriculum.

Your child will probably spend about five hours in total sitting the tests during one week in May. Most children do two papers in science and three papers each in mathematics and English.

Why are the tests important?

It is important that your child does as well as possible in these tests. It is not the purpose of the tests to help secondary schools to decide which children to give places to. But the results may be used to place your child in the appropriate teaching group. Remember that your child's work throughout Key Stage Two is also assessed by his or her teachers to give a clear picture of overall achievement.

What will my child do in the maths test?

Most children will take two written papers for Levels 3-5 in maths. One paper allows the use of a calculator, and one does not. The two papers contain the same number of marks. Each paper is 45 minutes long. Your child will also take a short mental arithmetic test. This will also count towards your child's final level in mathematics.

YOUR CHILD WILL BE TESTED ON THE FOLLOWING AREAS

- ✔ Number

- ✔ Shape, space and measure

- ✔ Handling data

The questions will also test the following skills:

- ✔ Knowledge and understanding

- ✔ Handling information

- ✔ Interpretation and evaluation

- ✔ Problem solving

What about children with different levels of ability?

If your child has a great deal of difficulty with maths he or she can do a practical task in a small group or individual basis with a teacher. This work is at a lower level than the written test but it allows any child in Year 6 to achieve a positive result.

Extension papers with Level 6 questions are available for exceptionally able pupils.

How do I know how well my child has done?

Your child's school sends the papers away for marking. You will receive:

- ✔ the results of your child's tests by the end of July

- ✔ a summary of the results for all pupils at the school

- ✔ a summary of results for pupils nationally

As with Key Stage One, the information you receive will help you compare your child's performance with that of other children of the same age. The report from your child's school will explain what the results show about your child's progress, strengths, particular achievements and targets for development. It may also explain how to follow up the results with your child's teachers.

Level 4 is the target level for children at the end of Key Stage Two.

What are the league tables?

Primary school performance (or league) tables are published annually. These show how your child's school has performed in the teacher assessments and tests compared to other schools locally and nationally.

How can I help my child prepare for the end of Key Stage Two assessment?

✔ Encourage your child to do the homework set and to discuss it with you.

✔ Help your child to practise answering written test-style questions – emphasise the importance of reading the question carefully and deciding what is actually being asked.

✔ Encourage your child to use techniques he or she has learnt to check work – using mental or written methods.

✔ Discuss why answers are right when practising questions.

✔ Encourage maths in situations other than practising for the tests.

How does my child's teacher assess performance?

Your child's teacher forms an overall picture of ability, strengths and achievements through several methods (see left). He or she then uses this information to decide what your child, and the class as a whole, needs to do next. This information is summarised in a report to you, normally once a year.

Remember: if you want to know how your child is doing, talk to his or her teacher. Together you can help your child achieve his or her full potential.

What is target setting?

The government has set national targets for schools based on the percentage of children achieving Level 4 and above in the end Key Stage assessments in English, mathematics and science. For maths, nationally, this figure is 75% of 11-year-olds reaching Level 4 or above by 2002. Individual education authorities set their own targets based on the results schools have been achieving. Individual schools also set targets by which they can measure progress from year to year. You can contact your child's school to find out their target for maths and the **Local Education Authority (LEA)** target.

Parent tip

"From a parent's point of view, the National Tests give an idea how your child is doing and you can compare that with what the average child is expected to do."

Calculators and computers

When should my child use a calculator?

You may worry that calculators 'do the sums' for your child or that using calculators can prevent children from learning or thinking. Calculators need to be used carefully but they can be a very useful tool in learning maths.

Children in the primary years are still developing mental calculation skills and written methods to solve problems. A calculator should not be used to replace these methods.

Calculators can be used for:

✔ learning about numbers and the number system
✔ predicting what will happen in a number problem
✔ playing games
✔ finding number patterns
✔ exploring larger numbers
✔ investigating fractions and decimals

Calculator skills

To make full use of a calculator's learning possibilities, your child will need to learn:

✔ in which order to press the keys

✔ how to key in amounts of money, fractions and measurements

✔ how to read the display

✔ how to use the memory

✔ how to use the constant key

Your child needs to learn when it is appropriate to use a calculator but mental calculation should always be the first choice. If your child does use a calculator he or she should be able to round numbers up and down and calculate mentally to gain a sense of the size of the answer. He or she can use techniques to check and repeat the calculation.

At what age will my child use a calculator?

In Key Stage One emphasis is placed on mental calculation and talking about maths. Children in Key Stage One may have access to calculators as a tool for individual exploration of numbers. Your child's school will probably introduce the children to calculators properly when they are in Key Stage Two.

By the end of Key Stage Two your child should be knowledgeable and competent in using calculators to solve problems with many steps.

> ### Parent quote
>
> "My daughter has realised that there are skills involved in using calculators and I encourage her to work out her own solutions to problems first."

Computers in mathematics

There are many software packages available to parents that focus on mathematics skills. Your child may also use mathematics software in school.

As with calculators, a computer is a tool to help your child learn – not to replace basic mental calculation skills. If your child has special needs a computer can be an essential aid to communication. Ask your child's teacher what software would be most appropriate for your child's individual needs.

Parent tips and quotes

"When working with your child ask questions, using mathematical vocabulary, and value the responses. Encourage your child to ask questions and explain what he or she is doing."

"The best way to find out if a child understands something is to ask him or her to explain it to you!"

"Some computer software programs are very useful as they can produce a wide range of examples for a particular topic."

"Some excellent educational software is available for maths, which my sons see as fun rather than work!"

"My daughter, Kayleigh, has enjoyed using computer software and I feel she has gained confidence and speed in solving problems. An adult is always nearby in case of a query!"

DO I NEED TO BUY A COMPUTER AND SPECIAL SOFTWARE?

Buying a computer is a very large investment and needs to be thought through carefully. A computer is not essential to improving your child's ability in maths, but if you do decide to buy one it can be very effective.

If you have a home computer, check what software is already available on it. There are many CD-ROMs and software packages to choose from in the shops. Before you buy, find out from other parents or teachers if they know anything about the software you have chosen. Ask if your child can experiment with it before you decide.

Most software teaches mathematics in a fun way but do guide your child through it carefully, ensuring he or she sees the purpose of the activity. There are also some websites on the Internet that have maths puzzles and problems suitable for children (some are listed on page 64 of this book).

Children can use computers to:

✔ explore, describe and explain number patterns – for example watching a counting 'meter' with sequences of numbers or looking at number grids

✔ practise and consolidate number skills by using software designed to teach or strengthen a particular skill

✔ explore and explain data and information – for example making, reading and interpreting tables, spreadsheets, pie charts and graphs

✔ experiment with patterns, movement and shapes – for example instructing a screen 'turtle' to move, rotating shapes or completing patterns

Home–school partnerships

How can I find out what my child is doing?

The communication between you and your child's school is very important for your child's success. Teachers need to meet and talk to you, and you need to talk to teachers and others involved in your child's education. Many parents are worried about talking to teachers because they may have had bad experiences themselves with maths. Don't be anxious – teachers are there to help!

Parent quotes

"I have found that becoming involved in my children's learning has helped with my own understanding of maths. I now feel much more confident helping my children with homework."

"My child's school provided a maths workshop evening. I realised that some other parents had the same anxieties about maths as I did. Talking helped and we now share ideas to help our children."

How to find out more

✔ Discuss with your child what he or she is doing in numeracy or maths.

✔ Look at any books or homework your child brings home and talk about them.

✔ Attend parents' evenings and open days.

✔ Read your child's home-school diary.

✔ Talk to other parents.

✔ Write a note to your child's teacher if you want to ask something.

✔ Make an appointment outside lesson time to talk to your child's teacher.

How can I help my child?

Schools and parents form partnerships with one common aim in mind – to help your child learn. Working together, not in opposition, will benefit your child.

How can I help the school?

✔ Offer to help in the classroom if you can spare the time.

✔ Offer to share a skill or expertise if you have one.

✔ Attend meetings and keep appointments.

✔ Collect resources that may be useful for your child's class, such as empty containers or objects for counting.

Remember, if you help the school, you are helping your child.

Tips

• Don't criticise the teacher or his or her teaching methods in front of your child.

• Don't constantly compare your child to brothers and sisters or other children at school.

What information will I receive from my child's school?

Just as children are different, so are schools. The type of information you are given may vary from school to school, so if there is something you would like to know that you have not been told – ask! Most schools operate an 'open door' policy, meaning that parents are welcome to speak to teachers when they need to. Remember not to interrupt a teacher when he or she is teaching!

Information you may receive

Information about your child:

- Annual reports, including information on individual subjects.
- Test results – school based tests, assessments or National Test scores.
- Progress reports throughout the year.
- Homework progress and marks.
- Completed workbooks, exercise books or activities.

Information about maths:

- Work to be covered each term.
- Lists of things children need to know, for example number bonds or times tables.
- If and when homework is given.
- Details about maths ability groups or sets.
- Timetables and details of lesson structure.
- List of equipment children may need (calculator, protractor etc.) if not provided by the school.

QUESTIONS TO ASK YOUR CHILD'S TEACHER:

1 Does my child seem happy and confident in numeracy lessons?

2 Does my child tackle problems independently or does he or she need help first?

3 Are there any areas of maths my child needs extra help with?

4 What exactly can I do at home to help with maths?

When you meet with your child's teacher it may be a chance to find out how they teach.

✔ Check that you understand the meanings of any unfamiliar mathematical words.

✔ Find out when homework is set and how you should be involved.

✔ Find out what particular methods are used.

✔ Look at any test and assessment results.

✔ Ask for any information you, as a parent, might find useful in order to help with maths.

Fun with numbers is what parents need to share with their children.

Glossary

Attainment Targets Targets for children's learning in each subject at different stages. Each attainment target is divided into eight levels, like steps up a ladder.

Baseline Assessment Teacher observation of children within the first seven weeks of entering the Reception class. It is used to assess learning levels in maths, English and social skills.

Capacity The capacity of a container is the amount of space inside it.

Core subjects The main subjects in the National Curriculum: English, maths and science. R.E. (religious education) and I.C.T. (Information and Communications Technology) are also treated like core subjects. These are the only subjects where set Programmes of Study have to be taught in full.

Data handling Collecting and organising information to display and use, for instance to make predictions.

Foundation subjects Subjects covered in schools as part of the National Curriculum which are not English, maths and science (the core subjects) or R.E. and I.C.T. These include history, geography, music, design technology, art and P.E.

Information and Communications Technology (I.C.T.) The term to replace I.T. (Information Technology) meaning the use of computers and other electronic means to enhance learning.

Key Stages Stages at which a child's education can be assessed, after following a programme of work. There are four Key Stages, dividing ages 5-7, 7-11, 11-14 and 14-16.

Local Education Authority (LEA) The city, county, borough or district education authority. LEAs have many specific roles especially in admissions, finance and special educational needs.

National Curriculum The government's system of education broken into four Key Stages, which applies to all pupils of compulsory school age in maintained schools. It contains core and foundation (non-core) subjects, and incorporates National Tests at the end of each Key Stage.

National Tests Tests taken in school at the end of each Key Stage – at ages 7, 11 and 14 – to determine what Attainment Target pupils have reached. The scores are also used, especially at age 11, to compare the results of schools as a whole.

Plenary The time at the end of the Daily Maths Lesson when a class gets together to discuss work they've just been doing in groups.

Teacher Assessment The teacher's own judgements about the level of progress children have made. This is both a part of deciding what and how to teach, and also takes place more formally at set times, especially with the National Tests at 7 and 11 years old.

Turtle A robot that can be controlled and made to move backwards, forwards and sideways. Mainly used by Key Stage One children.

USEFUL INFORMATION

Advisory Centre for Education (ACE)
Department A, Unit 1B Aberdeen Studios,
22 Highbury Grove London N5 2DQ
Web: www.ace-ed.org.uk
Phone: 020 7354 8321
Free advice, information and support for parents
of children in state schools.

Basic Skills Agency
7th Floor, Commonwealth House,
1-19 New Oxford Street London WC1A 1NU
Web: www.basic-skills.co.uk
Phone: 020 7405 4017
National development agency for basic literacy
and numeracy skills.

DfEE (Department for Education and Employment)
Sanctuary Buildings, Great Smith Street,
London SW1P 3BT
Web: www.dfee.gov.uk
Phone: 020 7925 5555

National Association for Special Educational Needs
NASEN House, 4/5 Amber Business Village,
Amber Close, Amington, Tamworth B77 4RP
Web: www.nasen.org.uk
Phone: 01827 311 500

National Confederation for Parent Teacher Associations (NCPTA)
2 Ebbsfleet Estate, Stonebridge Road,
Gravesend, Kent DA11 9DZ
Web: www.rmplc.co.uk/orgs/ncpta
Phone: 01474 560 618
Promotes partnership between home and
school, children, parents, teachers and education
authorities.

WEBSITES

www.forum.swarthmore.edu/students/elem
An American website, Math Forum, useful for finding out how children can learn mathematics, with activities and problems for 5-11 year olds.

www.ed.gov/pubs/parents
An American site with ideas on home education – Helping your Child learn Math.

www.hometown.aol.com/wiseowlsw
A UK children's specialist in education software to play online or download.

www.bbc.co.uk/education/schools/primary.shtml
Home and school learning resources for children. Try looking at Megamaths, Dynamo and Little Animals Activities Centre.

SOFTWARE

Anglia Multimedia – Primary Numeracy CD-ROMs Levels 1 and 3.
Web: www.anglia.co.uk

Cambridgeshire Software House – Amazing Maths CD-ROM.
Web: www.ourworld.compuserve.com/homepages/cshsoft
Phone: 01487 741223

LCL – CD-ROM Kids Maths (3-12 Years).
Web: lcl.co.uk

Topologika Software; 1 South Harbour; Harbour Village, Penryn, Cornwall TR10 8LR
Web: www.topolgka.demon.co.uk
Phone: 01326 377 771
A wide range of mathematics software covering number, control and data.